Must-Try Mer-*mazing* Recipes

Recipes

to Make at Home

BY

Christina Tosch

Copyright 2021 Christina Tosch

Copyright Notes

This Book may not be reproduced, in part or in whole, without explicit permission and agreement by the Author by any means. This includes but is not limited to print, electronic media, scanning, photocopying or file sharing.

The Author has made every effort to ensure accuracy of information in the Book but assumes no responsibility should personal or commercial damage arise in the case of misinterpretation or misunderstanding. All suggestions, instructions and guidelines expressed in the Book are meant for informational purposes only, and the Reader assumes any and all risk when following said information.

Table of Contents

Introduction 6

Sweet Snacks and Treats from Under the Sea 8

    Ariel's Chia Parfait 9

    Clam Shell Buttercream-Filled Cookies 11

    Enchanted Fudge 13

    Little Mermaid Glitter Pancakes 16

    Magical Mermaid Ice Cream 18

    Marbled Mermaid Donuts 21

    Marshmallow Mermaid Pie 24

    Mermaid Blondies 27

    Mermaid Breakfast Bagel 30

    Mermaid Cookie Pizza 32

    Mermaid Latte Oats with Caramelized Bananas 35

    Mermaid Mousse Cake 37

    Mermaid Muddy Buddies 41

    Mermaid Party Donuts with Candy Shells 43

Mermaid Popcorn 45

Mermaid Treasure Candy 47

Mermaid Yogurt Bites 50

Metallic Mermaid Bark 52

Mystical Mermaid Toast 55

No-Bake Mermaid Cake Bites 57

Ocean Blue Cheesecake 60

Sea-Maiden's Meringue Bites 63

Sea Nymph Tails 65

Sea Salt Ice Cream 67

Siren Smoothie Bowl 70

Siren's Spirulina Power Bites 72

Sparkling Mermaid Sugar Cones 74

Sweet FroYo Bark 76

Triton's Pop-Tart 78

Under the Sea Dessert Dip 80

Drinks from the Deep 82

Blue Lagoon Smoothie 83

Boozy Mermaid Jello Shots 85

Iced Mermaid Tea 89

Magical Mermaid Hot Chocolate 91

Mermaid Lemonade 93

Mermaid Milk 95

Mermaid White Wine 98

Siren's Smoothie 100

The Tipsy Mermaid 102

Vanilla Mermaid Smoothie 104

Author's Afterthoughts 106

About the Author 107

Introduction

Over the past 12-months, you couldn't go to a food court, coffee shop, or bakery without seeing unicorn or Frozen- themed food and drinks.

However, if you are now feeling underwhelmed by unicorns, passé about princesses, but misty-eyed about mystical mermaids, you are in the right place!

We've brought together a collection of some of the most magical and mystical mermaid recipes. A collection guaranteed to please not only kids but adults too!

Mermaid food is the latest Instagram craze, and the good news is, you can make it by adding simple ingredients to its easy-to-make recipes.

One of the ingredients, spirulina, is a superfood that you may not have come across before. It's this power that gives mermaid food its blue and green coloring.

Better yet, spirulina is a valuable source of protein, B vitamins, and iron.

This power is made using the dried blue-green alga, which you can source quite easily from health food stores. For flavor, always choose a good quality spirulina product.

Spirulina is perfect for all your mermaid-inspired recipes, including smoothies, smoothie bowls, puddings, and more.

Another great way to create mermaid-inspired recipes is to use shades of blue, green, purple food coloring drops and gels, pearl sprinkles, candy melts, frosting, candies, and more.

Whether you are planning a party or trying to get your kids to try something new, get in the swim with our 40 Must-Try Mer-*mazing* Mermaid Recipes.

Sweet Snacks and Treats from Under the Sea

Ariel's Chia Parfait

Your skin will glow like a mermaid's when you choose this healthy, fiber-rich parfait dessert.

Servings: 2-3

Total Time: 2hours 8min

Ingredients:

- 2 cups almond milk
- ½ cup chia seeds
- 1-2 tsp blue-green algae powder
- 1 tsp vanilla extract
- ½ tsp cinnamon
- ½-1 tbsp honey (to taste)
- 1 cup coconut or plain Greek yogurt
- Fresh fruit (of choice, to serve)
- Coconut flakes (for topping)

Directions:

At high speed, in a food blender, process the almond milk, chia seeds, algae powder, vanilla extract, and cinnamon, and sweeten with honey (to taste).

Transfer to the fridge to thicken for 2-8 hours.

Layer the pudding in a glass, alternating with the Greek yogurt.

Top with your favorite fresh fruit and coconut flakes.

Clam Shell Buttercream-Filled Cookies

These pretty clamshell buttercream-filled cookies are a quick way to create the perfect sweet treat for an under the sea or mermaid party.

Servings: 48

Total Time: 20min

Ingredients:

- ½ cup butter
- 2 cups icing sugar
- 1 tsp vanilla extract
- 2-3 tbsp cream
- Teal, blue, pink, and purple edible food dyes
- 24 store-bought vanilla cookies
- 24 large pearl sprinkles

Directions:

For the frosting, in a bowl, combine the butter with the icing sugar and vanilla extract.

Add the cream, beginning with 2 tablespoons, adding more until you achieve your preferred consistency.

Portion the mixture into 4 bowls. Dye each bowl a different color using the food dyes.

Portion each color into an icing bag with a star tip.

Swirl each color of frosting onto 6 cookies until you have 6 cookies of each color.

Add a pearl candy in front of each swirl of frosting.

Sandwich a second cookie onto each 'clam,' angling the top cookie to create a clam shape, and so you can easily see the hidden pearl inside.

Serve and enjoy.

Enchanted Fudge

This fudge is spell-binding and makes a pretty addition to any mermaid-inspired party table or birthday feast.

Servings: 16

Total Time: 4hours 25min

Ingredients:

- Nonstick cooking spray
- 3 cups white chocolate chips
- 1 (14 ounces) can sweetened condensed milk
- 1 tbsp butter
- 1 tsp vanilla extract
- Teal food coloring
- Violet food coloring
- Mermaid sprinkle mix, store-bought

Directions:

Using aluminum foil, line an 8" square baking pan. Spray the foil with nonstick cooking spray. Then, put it to one side.

Add the white chocolate chips and condensed milk to a pan, and continuously mix over moderate to low heat until the chips are nearly melted. Stir in the butter followed by the vanilla extract and continue stirring and heating until melted entirely.

Divide the mixture into 3 bowls.

Color one bowl of the mixture with teal food coloring and the other bowl with violet food coloring. Leave one bowl, plain.

Transfer the mixtures to the prepared baking pan in random scoops. Swirl them together with a blunt knife.

Top with sprinkles.

Tap the pan gently on the worktop to help remove any air bubbles.

Transfer to the fridge for approximately 4 hours.

Lift the aluminum foil from the pan, and remove the fudge from the foil.

Transfer the fudge to a chopping board, and using a knife, slice into 16 even squares.

Little Mermaid Glitter Pancakes

Sparkling and sweet, these pancakes are the best-ever breakfast or brunch for little mermaids everywhere!

Servings: 8-12

Total Time: 6min

Ingredients:

- 2 large eggs
- 10½ ounces flour
- 2½ cups semi-skimmed milk
- Blue food coloring (as needed)
- Vanilla extract (to taste, as needed)
- Edible glitter (as needed)
- Butter (as needed)
- Aerosol cream (to serve)

Directions:

First, in a bowl, whisk the eggs with the flour and milk.

When the mixture is smooth, add a drop of blue food coloring and vanilla extract (to taste), followed by a dusting of edible glitter.

On the stovetop, heat a frying pan. Add a little butter to the pan.

When the pan is hot, using a ladle, transfer the mixture from the bowl to the pan. Allow the batter to cook for 60 seconds or so before edging the mixture around the pancake's sides using a spatula. Flip the pancake over and transfer to a plate.

Then, squirt the aerosol cream down the middle of the pancake, scatter with more glitter.

Roll and enjoy.

Magical Mermaid Ice Cream

This colorful no-churn ice cream makes a magical sweet treat for everyone.

Servings: 12

Total Time: 8hours 15min

Ingredients:

- 2 cups heavy whipping cream
- 1 tsp vanilla extract
- 1 (14 ounces) can sweetened condensed milk
- Neon blue food coloring
- Purple food coloring
- Neon green food coloring
- Mermaid sprinkle mix, store-bought

Directions:

To a stand mixer bowl, add the cream with the vanilla extract and, on high speed, whisk for 2-3 minutes, until stiff peaks begin to form.

Add the condensed milk and continue whisking for another 60 seconds, scraping down the sides of the mixer bowl halfway through mixing.

Divide the mixture evenly until 3 separate bowls (1 bowl larger than the other 2).

To the larger bowl, add the blue food coloring, and to the other 2 smaller bowls, add the purple food coloring to one and the neon green food coloring to the other. Mix well to combine.

Place half of the blue into a casserole dish or loaf pan. Spoon dollops of half of the neon green and purple mixture, add the remaining blue, neon green, and purple. Firmly push the mixture into the loaf pan to expel any air bubbles. Using a spoon, smooth the top of the mixture.

Transfer to the freezer overnight.

Serve the ice cream with the mermaid sprinkle mix.

Marbled Mermaid Donuts

Candy seashells and gold sprinkles adorn these glazed homemade donuts.

Servings: 6

Total Time: 1hour 10min

Ingredients:

Donut Batter:

- 1 cup flour
- 1 tsp baking powder
- A pinch of salt
- 3 tbsp unsalted butter (melted)
- 2 tbsp runny honey
- ¼ cup sugar
- 1 egg
- 1 tsp vanilla
- ⅓ cup + 1 tbsp buttermilk
- Neon pink and purple blue candy melts

Mermaid Glaze:

- 3 tbsp whipping cream
- ½ cup powdered sugar
- Blue, pink, and purple food coloring
- Brown sugar
- Pearl-style candies or gumballs
- Silver star sprinkles

Directions:

For the batter: In a small bowl, whisk the flour with the baking powder and salt. Put to one side.

In a bowl, combine the butter with the runny honey, sugar, egg, and vanilla.

Stir in the buttermilk and mix well to incorporate.

Add the dry ingredients and mix, without over mixing, but until just combined.

Spoon the donut batter into an icing bag. Pipe the batter into a greased donut pan, and bake in the oven at 400 degrees F for 7 minutes. Allow to cool for 60 seconds while in the pan. Flip the pan over and remove the donuts. Allow the donuts to cool completely on a wire baking rack.

Pour the three candy melt colors into a shell-shaped chocolate mold.

Transfer the mold to the freezer for approximately 20 minutes until the candy melts have set.

For the mermaid glaze: In a bowl, whisk the whipping cream together with the powdered sugar, and whisk until incorporated.

Divide the glaze evenly into 3 small-size bowls and color the glaze with pink, purple and blue. Dollop each color into a larger size bowl.

One at a time, dunk and dip the donuts into the glaze. The marble pattern with the change, the more donuts you dunk. Then, arrange the donuts, in a single layer, on a wire baking rack.

Scatter a little brown sugar over the donuts to resemble sand. Decorate with pearl-style candies and silver star sprinkles.

Top with the chocolate shells and serve.

Marshmallow Mermaid Pie

Pretty, dreamy, and super creamy; a pie fit for a princess.

Servings: 6-8

Total Time: 2hours 25min

Ingredients:

- 1 store-bought single flaky pie crust
- 1 tsp gelatin powder
- ¼ cup water
- 2 egg whites (room temperature)
- ½ cup + 1 tbsp granulated sugar
- 4-5 drops green food coloring
- Coconut Whipped Cream:
- 1½ cups heavy whipping cream
- 1 tsp coconut extract
- Mini marshmallows, assorted pastel colors
- Shredded coconut (to serve)

Directions:

Using parchment paper or foil, cover the bottom and sides of the crust. Add baking beans and blind bake at 400 degrees F, for 30-40 minutes, until the crust is baked and the pie edges are golden.

In a small bowl, soak the gelatin powder in the water for 10 minutes. Next, using a double boiler, dissolve until clear. Allow to cool and put to one side.

For the pie: In a stand mixer, on low speed, whip the egg white, slowly increasing the speed to high. Once stiff peaks form, 1 teaspoon at a time, add the granulated sugar, process on moderate to high speed, until the sugar is combined.

Set the stand mixer to high speed, and slowly pour in the warm gelatin mixture.

Next, a couple of drops at a time, add the green food coloring until you achieve your preferred shade of mermaid green. Put to one side.

For the whipped cream, whip the cream with the coconut extract until it is the consistency of whipped cream. Put to one side.

When the crust is cool, spread the marshmallow pudding into the pastry crust. Transfer the pie to the refrigerator for 20 minutes to allow the pudding to set in the pie shell.

Take the pie out of the fridge, and spread the coconut whipped cream over the top.

Decorate the pie with mini marshmallows and shredded coconut.

Transfer to the fridge to chill for an additional 60 minutes.

Slice and serve.

Mermaid Blondies

Purple and teal food gels come together swimmingly to create these prettiest blondies ever!

Servings: 16

Total Time: 55min

Ingredients:

- 1 (16.25 ounces) box white cake mix
- ¼ cup vegetable oil
- 1 large egg (beaten)
- ¼-⅓ cup milk
- ½ cup white chocolate chips
- Teal food gel
- Purple food gel
- Frosting (as needed)
- Sprinkles (to decorate)

Directions:

First, preheat the main oven to 350 degrees F.

In a bowl, combine the white cake mix with the vegetable oil and beaten egg. Slowly add the milk, beginning with ¼ cup, adding more if necessary to create a thick, silky putty-like batter.

Add the white chocolate chips.

Transfer approximately 1 cup of batter to a small bowl. Add the purple food gel to the bowl, mixing until thoroughly combined.

Next, add the teal food gel to the remaining batter and transfer to an 8" square baking dish.

Spoon the purple batter onto the tea batter and, using a blunt knife, swirl to create an attractive design.

Bake in the oven for 25 minutes.

Then, remove from the oven. Cover with foil. Bake the blondies for an additional 15 minutes.

Remove the pan from the oven and allow to cool completely.

Once cooled, using a piping bag, drizzle the frosting over the blondies, decorate with sprinkles and serve.

Mermaid Breakfast Bagel

Indeed, things don't need to be fancy to be good! And your kids will love this fun mermaid-inspired breakfast bagel.

Servings: 1-2

Total Time: 4min

Ingredients:

- ¼ cup cream cheese (whipped)
- 1 plain bagel (halved and toasted)
- ¼ tsp blue-green spirulina

Directions:

Spread a light layer of whipped cream cheese on the cut side of both toasted bagel halves.

Sprinkle the spirulina over the cream cheese, and mix lightly to combine and create an attractive design.

Mermaid Cookie Pizza

This sweet dessert is pizza perfect for mermaid lovers everywhere!

Servings: 16

Total Time: 35min

Ingredients:

- Nonstick cooking spray
- 1 (16½ ounces) refrigerated chocolate chip cookie dough, 1 roll
- 1½ cups mini marshmallows
- 1 tub white frosting
- Violet food coloring
- Turquoise food coloring
- Mermaid sprinkles, store-bought
- White and blue round candy-coated chocolate candy

Directions:

First, preheat the main oven to 350 degrees F.

Using nonstick cooking spray, grease a 12" pizza pan.

Next, press the cookie dough into the pizza pan and bake until golden, for 12-15 minutes.

Add the mini marshmallows to the top of the cookie dough and bake for another 2-3 minutes, until the marshmallows puff up. Take out of the oven. Then, set aside to completely cool.

Set approximately ¼ cup of white frosting to one side.

Divide the remaining frosting into 2 even portions and transfer to 2 separate dishes.

Using the food coloring, color one dish purple, and the other turquoise.

Set 3 tablespoons of each aside in 2 small microwave-safe bowls for the drizzle.

Microwave both bowls of icing for 10 seconds, and stir until easy to pour. If it isn't, return to the microwave for 4-5 seconds. Mix thoroughly and drizzle over the pizza.

Decorate the pizza with mermaid sprinkles and candy chocolates.

Next, place a sheet of kitchen wrap on a flat work surface.

Spread each of the 3 colors of icing next to one another on the wrap, creating a 10-12" strip. Fold the kitchen wrap tightly and twist the ends.

Cut the tip of the kitchen wrap and place it in an icing bag, fitted with a star piping tip.

Pipe the icing onto the pizza's outer edge.

Mermaid Latte Oats with Caramelized Bananas

Get your little mermaids off to a great start with this healthy oat breakfast dish.

Servings: 2

Total Time: 8hours 4min

Ingredients:

- 1 tsp blue spirulina powder
- 1 tbsp coconut butter
- 1 cup coconut milk
- 1 cup steel-cut oats
- 1 tbsp coconut oil
- 1 banana (peeled and sliced)
- Maple syrup

Directions:

In a food blender, process the spirulina powder with the coconut butter and coconut milk until smooth, for 60 seconds.

Add the oats to a Mason jar.

Pour the mixture over the oats, seal, and allow to soak overnight.

In a pan, gently heat the coconut oil.

Dip the banana slices in the maple syrup and roast in the pan until golden.

Serve the oats with the caramelized bananas and enjoy.

Mermaid Mousse Cake

For the wow factor, invest in a shell-shape mold and create white chocolate shells to decorate this show-stopping cake.

Servings: 8-10

Total Time: 9hours 40min

Ingredients:

Cake:

- ⅓ cup sugar
- ⅓ cup all-purpose flour
- 3 tbsp cocoa powder
- ¼ tsp baking powder
- ¼ tsp bicarbonate of soda
- A pinch of salt
- ½ large egg (beaten)
- 2 tbsp milk
- 1 egg
- 1½ tbsp oil
- ¼ tsp vanilla
- 2 tbsp water

Mousse:

- 6 tsp gelatin
- 9 tbsp cold water
- 10 egg whites
- 1½ tsp vanilla extract
- 3⅓ cups whipping cream
- 1 tsp vanilla
- 1 cup milk
- 4½ cups white chocolate
- 2-3 drops blue food coloring

- White candy melts (melted)
- Cocoa powder (to dust)
- Blue sanding sugar (to decorate)
- White sprinkles (to decorate)
- White pearl nonpareils (to decorate)
- Pink jelly beans (to decorate)

Directions:

For the cake: Add the sugar, flour, cocoa powder, baking powder, bicarbonate of soda, and a pinch of salt in an electric mixer bowl, and on low speed, mix until combined.

Add the milk, egg, oil, vanilla extract, and water, and continue mixing until smooth.

Next, using parchment paper, line the bottom of a 10" springform pan. Pour the batter into the prepared pan, spreading it to the edges.

Bake in the oven at 350 degrees F, for 20-30 minutes, until springy to the touch.

Transfer the springform pan to a wire cooling rack and allow to completely cool.

Remove the cake from the pan along with the parchment paper.

Return the cake to the springform pan and put it to one side.

For the mousse: Scatter the gelatin into a small bowl of cold water. Then, put it to one side.

In a bowl, beat the egg whites until stiff peaks start to form.

Next, in a second bowl, combine the whipping cream with the vanilla and beat to form soft peaks.

Set both of the bowls to one side.

Over moderate heat, heat the milk. Just before it comes to a boil, turn the heat off, and add the gelatin, to dissolve. When dissolved, add the white chocolate and whisk until melted. It may be necessary to turn on the heat to achieve this. Add the mixture to the whipped cream, folding it in by hand.

Next, fold in the egg whites while maintaining the mixture's airy consistency.

Add 2-3 drops of blue coloring, gently folding to combine and create a marble effect.

Then, transfer the mousse into the pan and smooth the surface.

Put the pan on a large tray and transfer to the refrigerator to chill overnight. It is a good idea to crumple up a few kitchen paper towels around the pan to mop up any leakage.

Run a dampened, warm cloth around the sides of the pan, then carefully slide a sharp kitchen knife along the inside rim of the pan to loosen the cake. Unlatch the pan sides, and remove the cake from the pan.

Pour the melted white candy melts into a shell mold and transfer to the freezer for 15 minutes to set.

Dust the cake with a light coating of cocoa powder.

Decorate with blue sugar, sprinkles, jelly beans, chocolate shells, and pearl candies.

Slice, serve and enjoy.

Mermaid Muddy Buddies

Quick and easy to prepare, this no-bake sweet snack combines cereal with candy melts for pop-in-the-mouth perfection.

Servings: 6-8

Total Time: 45min

Ingredients:

- 1 cup turquoise blue candy melts
- 2-4 tbsp coconut oil (divided)
- 6 cups checkerboard square breakfast cereal
- 1⅓ cups confectioner's sugar
- 1 cup purple candy melts
- 1 cup dark blue candy melts

Directions:

Add ½ cup of turquoise blue candy melts in a microwave-safe bowl, and add ½ tablespoon of coconut oil and heat for 35 seconds. Stir to combine and reheat as needed in 10-second increments until no large chunks of candies remain. Add additional coconut oil to achieve a smooth texture.

Add 1½ cups of cereal to the melted candy melts, stirring coat.

Add ⅓ cup of confectioner's sugar in a ziploc bag. Add the candy-coated cereal to the bag. Seal the bag and shake well to ensure the cereal is covered with sugar.

Pour the muddy buddies in a thin layer onto a baking tray.

Repeat the process with each color.

Allow to dry and set for half an hour before mixing and serving.

Recipe

Mermaid Party Donuts with Candy Shells

If time is short, then this colorful party treat is ideal. Better yet, you can get your kids to help!

Servings: 12

Total Time: 15min

Ingredients:

- ⅓ cup vanilla candy wafers (melted)
- 1 (16 ounces) can vanilla frosting
- Blue food coloring
- Purple food coloring
- 12 store-bought donuts
- 3 tbsp sprinkles

Directions:

Melt the candy wafers and pour them into a shell-shaped mold. Then, transfer the mold to the fridge to set for 8-10 minutes. Remove from the mold and put aside.

Divide the frosting evenly between 2 microwave-safe bowls, and melt in 30 increments until creamy.

Add 3 drops of blue and 3 drops of purple food coloring to the melted frosting, and mix.

Dip the donuts in either the blue or purple frosting. Transfer the dipped donuts to a wire baking rack to allow any excess frosting to drip off.

Scatter over the sprinkles and add a candy shell to each one. Set the donuts aside for a minimum of 15 minutes.

Mermaid Popcorn

This popcorn is simple to make but coated in green candy and decorated with purple and pink gumballs, and it's a very effective 'under the sea' snack.

Servings: 4

Total Time: 12min

Ingredients:

- 5 cups popped popcorn
- 1½ cups blue candy melts
- 1½ tsp coconut oil
- ¼ cup green crystal sugar
- Candy-coated green shell candy (for topping)
- Purple and pink gum balls (to decorate)

Directions:

Using waxed paper, line a baking sheet.

Spread the popped corn over the baking sheet.

Next, add the candy melts and coconut oil to a microwave-safe bowl. In 30-second increments, microwave, stirring between intervals, until the candy is entirely melted.

Pour the melted candy over the popcorn, and stir to color the corn.

Lastly, decorate with green crystal sugar, green candy-shell coated candies and purple and pink gumballs. Enjoy.

Mermaid Treasure Candy

Rock this candy and discover a treasure trove of sparkling gems.

Servings: N/A*

Total Time: 3days 1hour 15min

Ingredients:

- 10½ ounces granulated sugar
- 4/5 cup water
- 1 tsp agar powder
- A dash of pink food coloring
- A dash of violet food coloring
- A dash of teal food coloring

Directions:

First, in a pan, combine the sugar with the water and agar powder, and bring to boil. Continue heating for 5 minutes.

Transfer the mixture into a parchment-lined loaf pan.

Dip a brush in the pink food coloring and swirl it into the mixture on the far left of the pan.

Dip a second brush in the violet food coloring and swirl it into the mixture in the middle of the pan.

Dip a third brush in the teal food coloring and swirl it into the mixture on the far right of the pan.

Next, transfer to the fridge to set for around 60 minutes.

Remove the pan from the fridge and remove the gem mixture.

Transfer the gem mixture to a new parchment-lined pan.

Using clean hands, treat the gem mixture into random pieces.

Then, spread the pieces in a single layer, and not touching one another on a tray. Allow the gems to dry for 3-4 days in a well-ventilated environment.

*Servings will depend on the size of the candy

Mermaid Yogurt Bites

These yogurt bites are a healthy yet fun-size snack or treat. Better yet, this recipe is something everyone can help create.

Servings: 16

Total Time: 3hours 6min

Ingredients:

- 2 cups vanilla yogurt
- Lime green food coloring (as needed)
- Neon purple food coloring (as needed)
- Electric blue food coloring (as needed)
- Gold cake dust (as needed)

Directions:

Divide the yogurt between 3 individual bowls.

Add 2 drops of each of the food coloring to each bowl and stir to combine.

Using a spoon, layer a little of each color yogurt (green, purple, and blue) into each ice cube tray section. Scatter gold dust over the yogurt and place it in the freezer for 3 hours.

Remove from the freezer and remove from the ice cube tray.

Serve at once.

Metallic Mermaid Bark

Silver sprinkles and edible gold dust decorate this delicious candy bark.

Servings: 12

Total Time: 25min

Ingredients:

- 12 ounces bright white candy melts
- 12 ounces turquoise candy melts
- 12 ounces purple candy melts
- Pink, blue and purple round chocolate shimmer candies (various sizes)
- Silver sprinkles
- Edible gold disco dust

Directions:

First, pour each color of candy melts into their own individual microwave-safe bowl.

Microwave each bowl of candy, melts, for 30 seconds, and stir until smooth.

Microwave for an additional 30 seconds, and stir until smooth.

Using waxed paper, line a baking sheet.

Next, make dollops of each candy melt color in mounds all over the baking sheet.

With a spatula, stir the colors together and spread the candy to the baking sheet's edges. Aim not to over mix the colors as they should be swirled rather than combined entirely.

Scatter the chocolate shimmer candies over the bark, followed by the silver sprinkles and edible gold disco dust.

Next, transfer the bard to the fridge until set, for 15 minutes.

Remove the bark from the waxed paper, and with clean hands, break the bark into random pieces.

Place in the fridge until you are ready to serve.

Mystical Mermaid Toast

Your kids will rush downstairs for breakfast when you add this mermaid-inspired toast to your weekly menu.

Servings: 4

Total Time: 8min

Ingredients:

- 4 slices sandwich bread
- 7 ounces cream cheese
- 2-3 drops blue food coloring
- 2-3 drops green food coloring
- 2-3 drops pink food coloring
- A pinch of blue-green spirulina
- A pinch of edible silver glitter

Directions:

First, toast the bread until golden on both sides.

Keep half of the cream cheese plain and divide the remaining cream cheese into 3 equal portions. Using the food coloring, create 3 different cream cheese colors.

Spread an even layer of the uncolored cream cheese on each slice of toast. Top with a layered of cream cheese, and top with a sprinkle of blue-green spirulina.

Then, using a palette knife, evenly spread and dust with glitter.

No-Bake Mermaid Cake Bites

If you are bored with baking and looking for a speedy sweet treat, these no-bake mermaid cake bites are the way to go.

Servings: 12

Total Time: 35min

Ingredients:

Cake Batter:

- 8 tbsp butter
- 1 tsp vanilla extract
- 1 tsp green spirulina
- 1 tsp blue spirulina
- 1½ cups yellow cake mix
- ½ cup flour
- ¼ cup cane sugar

Cocoa Butter Shell:

- 2 ounces cocoa butter
- ½ cup confectioner's sugar
- 1 tsp butterfly pea powder
- 1 tsp coconut flour
- A pinch of salt

Vanilla Lemon Icing:

- 1 tsp apple cider vinegar
- 1 tbsp freshly squeezed lemon juice
- 1 tsp vanilla extract
- ½ cup confectioner's sugar
- ¼ cup coconut oil (softened)

Directions:

In a bowl, combine the batter ingredients (butter, vanilla extract, green spirulina, blue spirulina, yellow cake mix, flour, and cane sugar). Using a fork, slowly work in the butter. You may want to add 1 tablespoon of coconut oil or additional butter if the batter is too dry.

When the mixture is the correct consistency, roll the mixture into balls, and transfer to the freezer.

Over low heat, melt the cocoa butter, remove from the stovetop and keep at room temperature.

Work in the confectioner's sugar, slowly and a little at a time. Add the remaining ingredients; butterfly pea powder, coconut flour, and a pinch of salt.

Prepare the icing. Add the vinegar, lemon juice, vanilla extract, confectioner's sugar, and softened coconut oil to a bowl and mix to combine.

Spoon the cocoa butter mixture over the cake bites to coat and return to the freezer for 20 minutes.

Remove from the freezer, and drizzle with the vanilla lemon icing and serve.

Ocean Blue Cheesecake

Bring the sand and sea to your dining table with this ocean blue cheesecake.

Servings: 6

Total Time: 8hours 25min

Ingredients:

Base:

- 1½ cups almond meal
- 2 tbsp rice malt syrup
- 2 tbsp coconut oil (melted)
- ⅛ tsp salt

Topping:

- 1 cup raw cashews
- ¼ cup white solid parts of canned coconut cream (chilled)
- ¼ cup coconut flavor yogurt
- ½ cup pure maple syrup
- ¼ cup coconut oil (melted and warmed)
- ¼ cup freshly squeezed lemon juice
- Zest of 1 medium lemon
- 1 tsp vanilla
- 1-2 tsp blue spirulina
- Ground peanuts (to decorate)
- ¼ cup green rock candy (to decorate)
- ¼ cup blue rock candy (to decorate)

Directions:

First, add the base ingredients (almond meal, rice malt syrup, coconut oil, and salt) and mix thoroughly to create a sticky, crumbly mixture.

Second, press the mixture into the bottom of a pie pan and place it in the freezer while preparing the filling.

Soak the cashews overnight.

Add the raw cashews, white parts of canned coconut cream, coconut yogurt, maple syrup, coconut oil, lemon juice, lemon zest, and vanilla extract to a food blender. Process until lump-free and smooth and creamy. Pour out half of the mixture and put to one side.

In one half, add the blue spirulina and mix to combine.

Add dollops of the white mixture and blue mixture to the pan, alternating between the two to create layers of contrasting colors. Take a skewer and swirl them to make an attractive design.

Next, transfer to the freezer to set for 8 hours.

When entirely set, decorate with ground peanuts to resemble sand and decorate with rock candy.

Allow the cheesecake to thaw at room temperature for several minutes before enjoying it.

Sea-Maiden's Meringue Bites

Pop-in-the-mouth melting perfection, these meringue bites are ideal for a baby shower, kid's party, or mermaid-theme event. What's more, you can use different flavor extracts and food colorings to suit your color scheme.

Servings: 4-6

Total Time: 1hour 15min

Ingredients:

- 2 egg whites
- 1 cup confectioner's sugar (divided)
- ⅛ tsp cotton candy extract
- Blue, pink, and purple food coloring

Directions:

Preheat the main oven to 175 degrees F.

Beat the egg whites until stiff on high speed until stiff peaks begin to form, for approximately 5 minutes.

Next, add ½ cup of confectioner's sugar and beat until stiff and glossy, for around 5 minutes.

Fold in the remaining sugar and cotton candy extract until incorporated fully.

Separate the meringue into 3 individual bowls. Then, add 2-3 drops of blue food coloring to one bowl, 2-3 drops of pink food coloring to the second bowl, and 2-3 drops of purple food coloring to the third, gently folding into the meringue.

Fill 3 piping bags fitted with a tri-color coupler with each color.

Pipe the meringue into small piles on a cookie sheet lined with parchment paper.

Then, bake the meringue in the preheated oven for 60-90 minutes, until dry to the touch.

Allow to cool and enjoy.

Sea Nymph Tails

These blue and violet chocolate-covered pretzel rods decorated with nonpareils, sprinkles and sanding sugar are ideal for a bake sale, edible gift, or party treat.

Servings: 10-12

Total Time: 15min

Ingredients:

- 1 cup white chocolate melting wafers (divided)
- Blue food coloring
- Violet food coloring
- Pretzel rods
- Silver nonpareils
- Blue and purple sanding sugar
- Violet sprinkles

Directions:

First, in a microwave-safe bowl, melt the white chocolate wafer in the microwave and according to the package instructions.

Divide the mixture evenly into 2 cups. Add the blue food coloring to one cup and purple food coloring to the other.

Next, dip the pretzel rods, approximately halfway, into the blue chocolate, turning to coat evenly.

Drip and drizzle the violet melted chocolate attractively over the blue chocolate.

Arrange the rods on a wax paper sheet and decorate with silver nonpareils, dust with blue and purple sanding sugar and scatter over violet sprinkles.

Allow to dry and serve in a Mason jar.

Sea Salt Ice Cream

Add a salty kick to this creamy mermaid-inspired ice cream with a sprinkling of sea salt.

Servings: 4

Total Times: 3hours 45min

Ingredients:

- 2 eggs
- ⅓ cup sugar
- 2 cups whole milk
- Sea salt
- 1 cup heavy cream
- 1 tsp vanilla extract
- 12 drops blue food coloring
- 3 drops green food coloring

Directions:

First, separate the egg into 2 large bowls.

Beat the whites until stiffened.

Add the sugar to the yolks until thickened.

Over moderate heat, bring the milk slowly to the bowl while occasionally stirring.

Pour the hot milk into the egg yolk-sugar mixture and mix thoroughly.

Return the milk-egg yolk-sugar mixture into the pan and, on moderate heat, heat until thickened to a custard-like consistency.

Pour the custard into the beaten egg whites and mix thoroughly.

Adding a little at a time, add the sea salt to taste.

Transfer the mixture to the refrigerator to cool.

When cool, add the cream and vanilla extract.

Swirl in the blue and green food coloring.

Transfer the mixture to your ice cream maker and churn according to the manufacturer's directions.

Siren Smoothie Bowl

This protein-packed smoothie bowl is packed full of superfoods, making it perfect for lustrous hair and clear skin. What more could a mermaid ask for?!

Servings: 1-2

Total Time: 4hours 12min

Ingredients:

- 3 ripe bananas
- ½ ripe avocado (peeled, pitted, and chopped)
- ¼ cup unsweetened vanilla nut milk (of choice)
- 1 scoop vanilla flavor protein powder
- ½ tsp spirulina powder

Toppings:

- Chia seeds
- Toasted coconut flakes
- Fruit (of choice)
- Granola

Directions:

Slice and freeze the bananas for a minimum of 4 hours before preparing the smoothie bowl.

Next, take the frozen bananas out of the freezer and allow them to sit on the worktop to defrost a little, for 6-8 minutes.

In a food blender, slowly pulse and blend the bananas with the avocado, vanilla nut milk, protein powder, and spirulina powder. Blend until creamy, thickened, and an ice cream consistency. This process will take 2-3 minutes.

Then, transfer the smoothie mixture to a bowl and top with chia seeds, coconut flakes, fresh fruit, and granola.

Siren's Spirulina Power Bites

Mermaids are strong, independent, and powerful, which is why these power bites are the perfect pop-in-the-mouth sweet snack for all would-be sirens!

Servings: 15-20

Total Time: 5min

Ingredients:

- 1 cup dates (pitted)
- ½ cup raisins
- ¾ cup almonds
- 2 tbsp blue-green spirulina
- 3 tsp freshly squeezed lemon juice

Directions:

Add the dates, raisins, almonds, spirulina, and lemon juice to a food processor and process until fully incorporated.

Using clean hands, roll the mixture into even-size balls, and store in the fridge for up to 10 days.

Sparkling Mermaid Sugar Cones

Who could resist these sparkling mermaid ice cream cones? Add your favorite flavor of ice cream and enjoy.

Servings: 12

Total Time: 5min + drying time

Ingredients:

- ½ cup white candy melts
- ½ cup teal candy melts
- ½ cup violet candy melts
- 3 tsp canola oil (divided)
- 12 sugar cones
- Pearl dust (to decorate)
- Ice cream, store-bought (to serve, of choice)
- Silver and gold glitter sprinkles (to decorate)

Directions:

In 3 microwave-safe bowls, melt each color of candy melts, adding 1 teaspoon of canola oil to each color, until melted entirely. Stir to combine.

In a small bowl, drop the candy melts, marbling the chocolate.

Dip each cone into the dish, tapping off any excess gently. Allow to dry completely.

Using clean food-safe brushes, brush with pearl dust.

Transfer the cones to a resealable container.

Serve with ice cream and decorate with silver and gold glitter sprinkles.

Sweet FroYo Bark

Homemade candy tastes way better than any you can buy in the store, and better yet, it's better for you too, with a lot less sugar and additives.

Servings: N/A*

Total Time: 2hours 15min

Ingredients:

- 1½ cups fat-free Greek yogurt
- ¼ cup runny honey
- 1 cup mermaid sprinkles
- 1 cup white chocolate chips (separated)

Description:

First, in a bowl, combine the yogurt with the runny honey until combined thoroughly.

Using a spatula, fold in ½ cup of the white chocolate chips, followed by ½ cup of mermaid sprinkles.

Line a ¼ sheet baking pan with parchment paper.

Spoon the yogurt mixture into the pan, smoothing it out to create an even layer.

Next, sprinkle the remaining white chocolate chips over the yogurt mixture, followed by the remaining mermaid sprinkles.

Put the pan in the freezer for at least 2-3 hours, until chilled.

Remove the pan from the freezer and break the bark into random pieces.

Store the bark in the freezer until you ready to serve.

*Servings will indeed depend on the size of the bark pieces

Triton's Pop-Tart

We bet Triton, the mighty merman son of the god of the sea, Poseidon, and the goddess of the sea, Amphitrite, would agree, this pop tart is heavenly!

Servings: 2

Total Time: 20min

Ingredients:

- 1 sheet ready-made puff pastry
- 4 spoonfuls strawberry jam
- Blue, royal icing (as needed)
- Sprinkles (as needed)
- Nonpareils white pearls (to decorate)

Directions:

Place the pastry on a cutting board, horizontally.

Cut the pastry into 4 even-size rectangles.

Add 2 spoonfuls of jam on 2 of the pastry rectangles.

Lay the plain pastry rectangles on top of the jam. Using a metal fork, crimp the edges to seal.

Bake in the oven at 350 degrees F for 15 minutes, until golden.

Using the icing, make a wave of frosting across the surface of each pop tart.

Scatter over the sprinkles and decorate with pearl candies.

Under the Sea Dessert Dip

If you are planning a mermaid-themed party, you will be looking to make lots of sweet treats and snacks, and this dessert dip is perfect because you can have lots of fun using different food colorings and sprinkles.

Servings: 6-8

Total Time: 10min

Ingredients:

- 8 ounces cream cheese
- 16 ounces marshmallow fluff
- 1½ ounces vanilla pudding mix
- 1 tsp vanilla extract
- 1 tsp salt
- 1 tbsp cream
- 1 drop blue food coloring
- 1 drop neon green food coloring
- 1 drop purple food coloring
- Sprinkles (to decorate)
- Cookies (to serve, optional)
- Pretzels (to serve, optional)
- Fresh fruit, chopped (to serve, optional)

Directions:

Add the cream cheese to a stand mixer and combine with the marshmallow fluff, vanilla pudding mix, vanilla extract, and salt. Once the ingredients are incorporated, add the cream to loosen the consistency.

Divide the mixture into 3 individual bowls, and add one food coloring to each bowl.

Pour the colored mixtures into one large bowl, directly layering one on top of the other. Using a cocktail stick, swirl the colors.

Add the sprinkles and serve with cookies, pretzels, and chunks of fresh fruit.

Drinks from the Deep

Blue Lagoon Smoothie

This Instagram-worthy smoothie is undoubtedly something to post about!

Servings: 2

Total Time: 5min

Ingredients:

- 2 large bananas
- 1½ cups plain, non-fat Greek yogurt
- 2 tbsp unsweetened coconut flakes
- 2 tsp spirulina
- 2 tbsp chia seeds
- 2 tbsp fresh blueberries
- 6 tbsp coconut water
- Dried coconut flakes (to garnish)
- 2 kiwis (peeled and sliced, to garnish)
- Fresh blueberries (to garnish)
- Chia seeds (to garnish)

Directions:

In a food blender, combine the bananas, yogurt, coconut flakes, spirulina, chia seeds, fresh blueberries, and coconut water. Process until smooth.

Pour the smoothie into two chilled glasses. Then, top with coconut flakes, kiwi slices, blueberries, chia seeds.

Boozy Mermaid Jello Shots

These boozy jello shots may be a little time-consuming to prepare, but with their show-stopping colorful mermaid layers, they are well worth the effort!

Servings: 18

Total Time: 9hours 30min

Ingredients:

Jello Layer:

- 1 (3 ounces) sachet purple grape gelatin powder
- 3 cups boiling water (divided)
- ½ cup coconut rum (divided)
- 1½ cups cold water (divided)
- 1 (3 ounces) sachet berry blue gelatin powder
- 1 (3 ounces) lime green gelatin powder

White Layer:

- 1 (14 ounces) can sweetened condensed milk
- 1½ cups boiling water
- ½ cup cold water
- 2 (3 ounces) envelopes unflavored gelatin powder

Whipped Cream:

- 2 cups heavy whipping cream
- ½ cup powdered sugar
- 2 tsp vanilla essence
- Blue food coloring
- Blue sprinkles (to garnish)

Directions:

First, prepare the jello layer. Dissolve the grape gelatin powder in 1 cup of boiling water. Stir in 2 tbsp rum and ½ cup cold water until combined. Divide the mixture between 18 plastic cups and chill for 2 hours, until set.

Next, dissolve the berry blue gelatin powder in 1 cup of boiling water. As before, stir in 2 tbsp coconut rum and ½ cup cold water. Set aside.

Finally, dissolve the lime green gelatin powder in 1 cup of boiling water. Stir in 2 tbsp coconut rum and ½ cup cold water. Set aside.

Now, prepare the white layer. In a jug, whisk together the condensed milk and 1 cup boiling water.

Add the cold water to a small bowl and sprinkle over the unflavored gelatin. Allow to sit for a couple of minutes. Stir in ½ cup boiling water to dissolve the gelatin. Add this to the condensed milk and stir until combined. Set aside until cooled to room temperature,

Take the plastic cups out of the refrigerator. Spoon an even layer of the milk mixture into each plastic cup, on top of the purple layer. Chill for half an hour.

Now, pour an even layer of the prepared blue jello over the milk layer. Chill for 1-2 hours until set.

Spoon another layer of the milk mixture over the set blue layer. Chill for half an hour.

Spoon an even layer of the prepared green jello over the last white layer. Chill for 1-2 hours.

Next, spoon another layer of the milk mixture over the set green layer. Chill for half an hour.

Finish with a layer of blue jello. Keep in the refrigerator until completely set.

Ten or so minutes before you are ready to serve the jello shots, prepare the whipped cream. Using an electric whisk, whip the cream with the powdered sugar and vanilla essence until it can hold stiff peaks. Add enough blue food coloring to achieve your desired shade, and whisk until combined.

Lastly, transfer the whipped cream to a piping bag and swirl on top of each jello shot portion. Finish with a garnish of blue sprinkles and serve.

Iced Mermaid Tea

Lavender syrup pairs perfectly with the floral notes in aromatic earl grey tea. Not to mention, it gives this soothing blend a delightful pastel purple hue that any mermaid would approve of.

Servings: 3

Total Time: 12min

Ingredients:

- 2 earl grey tea bags
- ¾ cup boiling water
- 2 tsp honey
- 2 tbsp lavender-flavored syrup
- 1 tbsp half & half
- 1 cup ice

Directions:

Add the tea bags, boiling water, honey, lavender syrup, and half & half to a glass, stir gently to combine. Allow to steep for 3-4 minutes.

Squeeze the tea bags and then remove them from the glass.

Add the ice to the glass, stir once again, and serve.

Magical Mermaid Hot Chocolate

Make a mug of hot chocolate more magical with blue coloring and colored sprinkles.

Servings: 3

Total Time: 12min

Ingredients:

- 1½ cups whole milk
- 1½ cups half & half
- 4 ounces good-quality white baking chocolate (broken)
- ½ tsp vanilla extract
- 1 drop edible blue coloring
- Whipped cream (to serve)
- Colored sprinkles (to serve)

Directions:

Over moderate heat, while frequently stirring and without boiling, combine the milk with the half & half, baking chocolate, and vanilla extract. When the chocolate is melted and the mixture is hot, take the pan off the heat.

Add the blue coloring and stir to combine.

Pour the hot chocolate into mugs and top with whipped cream and colored sprinkles.

Enjoy!

Mermaid Lemonade

Everyone will love this lemonade! It's sweet, colorful, and mer-mazing!

Servings: 3

Total Time: 5min

Ingredients:

- 3 cups filtered water (room temperature)
- Freshly squeezed juice of ½ lemon
- 1 tbsp apple or coconut cider vinegar
- 1–2 tsp pure maple syrup
- ⅛–¼ tsp spirulina powder
- Ice cubes

Directions:

Pour the water into a Mason jar. Then, whisk in the lemon juice, vinegar, maple syrup, and ⅛ teaspoon of spirulina powder to combine. Add more spirulina powder until you achieve your preferred shade of blue-green.

Add a handful of ice cubes.

Shake well or stir to prevent the spirulina from settling.

Mermaid Milk

Delectably take your snack time to the next level! What is a better drink to serve with your homemade cookies than this sweet and delicious mermaid milk?

Servings: 1-2

Total Time: 10min

Ingredients:

- A handful of ice
- 3 scoops vanilla ice cream
- ½ cup whole milk
- 1-2 drops mint blue food coloring
- Pastel-colored sprinkles (to garnish)

Whipped Cream:

- ½ cup heavy whipping cream
- 1 tsp vanilla extract
- 1 tbsp confectioner's sugar
- 1 drop pink food coloring
- 1 drop mint blue food coloring

Directions:

Add the ice, vanilla ice cream, milk, and mint blue food coloring in a food blender, and process until creamy.

For the whipped cream, add the heavy whipping cream, vanilla extract, and confectioner's sugar in a bowl.

Use a hand mixer. Then, whip until fluffy and light.

Fold the pink into the mint blue food coloring to create purple.

Fold in purple food coloring.

Garnish with pastel-colored sprinkles.

Serve and enjoy.

Mermaid White Wine

Plain old white wine won't do for a mermaid! Transform your mermaid into an under-the-sea treat with vibrant blue curacao, vanilla frosting, and sprinkles rim!

Servings: 1

Total Time: 5min

Ingredients:

To Rim:

- 3 tbsp vanilla frosting
- 2 tbsp sugar sprinkles (teal, purple and pink mixture)
- 2 tbsp brown sugar
- 1 pearl candy

Cocktail:

- 5 ounces white wine
- 1 ounce blue curaçao
- 2 drops pure vanilla extract

Directions:

First, rim the glass: Dip the rim of a large wine glass in a fine layer of white vanilla frosting. Immediately roll the frosting in the tri-color sugar sprinkles.

Spread the frosting around the base of the wine glass. Dip in brown sugar and set aside for 60 seconds. Use the icing as you would glue, and stick the candy pearl to the glass base to decorate.

For the cocktail, combine the white wine, blue *curaçao,* and vanilla extract in the wine glass and serve chilled.

Siren's Smoothie

One thing is for sure when you prepare this smoothie, you will be going a long way towards your 5-a-day!

Servings: 1

Total Time: 4min

Ingredients:

- 1 cup frozen mango chunks
- 1 ripe, large frozen banana
- 1½-2 cups almond milk
- ½ cup English cucumber
- 1-2 tsp blue-green algae powder
- 2 Medjool dates (pitted)

Directions:

Add the mango, banana, 1½ cups of almond milk, cucumber, blue-green algae powder (to color), and dates to a food blender. Process until silky smooth. You may want to add more almond milk to thin out the consistency.

Serve and enjoy.

The Tipsy Mermaid

Color this fruity pina colada with spirulina to give it a tempting mermaid twist.

Servings: 2

Total Time: 6min

Ingredients:

- 4 ounces white rum
- 1 (14 ounces) can coconut milk
- 1 tsp spirulina
- 2 cups ice
- 3½ cups frozen pineapple
- 2 pineapple wedges (to garnish)

Directions:

In a food blender, at high speed, blend the rum, coconut milk, spirulina, ice, and frozen pineapple until combined.

Then, pour the drink into glasses. Garnish with a wedge of fresh pineapple.

Vanilla Mermaid Smoothie

Start the day with this mermaid smoothie, and make sure your day goes swimmingly well!

Servings: 1

Total Time: 6min

Ingredients:

- ¼ cup vanilla protein powder
- 1 small size frozen banana
- 2 tbsp quick-cooking oats
- 1 tbsp runny honey
- 1 tsp spirulina
- 1 tsp white chia seeds
- ¾ cup unsweetened almond milk
- 1 tsp toasted coconut flakes
- ½ small kiwi (peeled and sliced)
- 2 tbsp fresh blueberries

Directions:

Add the vanilla protein powder with the banana, oats, honey, spirulina, chia seeds, and almond milk and in a food blender process until smooth.

Pour the smoothies into a tall glass, garnish with coconut flakes, kiwi slices, and fresh blueberries.

Serve and enjoy.

Author's Afterthoughts

I would like to express my deepest thanks to you, the reader, for making this investment in one my books. I cherish the thought of bringing the love of cooking into your home.

With so much choice out there, I am grateful you decided to Purch this book and read it from beginning to end.

Please let me know by submitting an Amazon review if you enjoyed this book and found it contained valuable information to help you in your culinary endeavors. Please take a few minutes to express your opinion freely and honestly. This will help others make an informed decision on purchasing and provide me with valuable feedback.

Thank you for taking the time to review!

Christina Tosch

About the Author

Christina Tosch is a successful chef and renowned cookbook author from Long Grove, Illinois. She majored in Liberal Arts at Trinity International University and decided to pursue her passion of cooking when she applied to the world renowned Le Cordon Bleu culinary school in Paris, France. The school was lucky to recognize the immense talent of this chef and she excelled in her courses, particularly Haute Cuisine. This skill was recognized and rewarded by several highly regarded Chicago restaurants, where she was offered the prestigious position of head chef.

Christina and her family live in a spacious home in the Chicago area and she loves to grow her own vegetables and herbs in the garden she lovingly cultivates on her sprawling estate. Her and her husband have two beautiful children, 3 cats, 2 dogs and a parakeet they call Jasper. When Christina is not hard at work creating beautiful meals for Chicago's elite, she is hard at work writing engaging e-books of which she has sold over 1500.

Make sure to keep an eye out for her latest books that offer helpful tips, clear instructions and witty anecdotes that will bring a smile to your face as you read!

Printed in Great Britain
by Amazon